GRACE NOTES:

NEW AND SELECTED POEMS

Grace Notes

New and Selected Poems

Eugene McNamara

For Robert Hill —
in admiration

All Best

Eugene McNamara
MAY, '05

Black Moss Press
2004

National Library of Canada Cataloguing in Publication

McNamara, Eugene, 1930-
    Grace notes : new and selected poems / Eugene McNamara.

ISBN 0-88753-390-6

    I. Title.

PS8575.N34G73 2004   C811'.54   C2004-901863-9

Some of these poems have appeared previously in *Canadian Forum, Windsor Review, Poetry Canada, The Glass Cherry, Ontario Review, Antigonish Review, Literary Review of Canada, Queens Quarterly, Poetry Toronto, Cross Canada Writers Quarterly, Writ* and *Northland Review*. Some were collected in the following anthologies and books: *I Want to be the Poet of Your Kneecaps* (ed John B Lee, Black Moss Press, 1999) *Following the Plough* (ed John B Lee, Black Moss Press, 2001), *The Dominion of Love* (ed Tom Wayman, Harbour, 2001) *Forcing the Field* (Sesame Press, l982) *The Moving Light* (Wolsak and Wynn, 1986) *Keeping in Touch* (Mosaic Press, 1998) and *Grace Notes* (Permission Press, 2001). "Matins" was set for choir and piano by John Burge and premiered in Windsor by the Windsor Classic Chorale on May 7, 2000. "For Roy Orbison" a film by Michael McNamara (Queen West Productions, 1999) was aired on Bravo! in 2000. "Mountains and Rivers Without End" was set for choir and piano by Christopher Kovarik and premiered in Windsor by the University of Windsor Chamber Choir on April 6, 2003.

Grateful thanks must be given to the editors, publishers, composers and film-makers listed here.

Author photo by David Fine. Cover design by Christopher McNamara

Published by Black Moss Press at 2450 Byng Road, Windsor, Ontario N8W 3E8. Black Moss books are distributed by Firefly Books, 66 Leek Crescent, Richmond Hill, ON Canada L4B 1H1. U.S. orders should be directed to Firefly Books at 4 Daybreak Lane, Westport, CT U.S.A. 06880-2157.

Black Moss gratefully acknowledges the generous support given by the Canada Council for the Arts and the Ontario Arts Council for its publishing program.

ONTARIO ARTS COUNCIL
CONSEIL DES ARTS DE L'ONTARIO

Le Conseil des Arts | The Canada Council
du Canada | for the Arts

For Margaret

Always—

Heaven is under our feet as well as over our heads.
—Thoreau

I have seen these ways of God: I know of no reason
For fire and change and torture and the old returnings
He being sufficient might be still. I think they admit no reason
        They are the ways of my love.
Unmeasured power, incredible passion, enormous craft: No
        Thought outside itself: a certain measure in phenomena:
The fountains of the boiling stars, the flowers on the foreland,
        The ever-returning roses of dawn.

—Robinson Jeffers

AUTHOR NOTE

Eugene McNamara was born in Oak Park, Illinois. After attending Northwestern University where he received his PhD he emigrated to Canada and taught American Literature and Creative Writing at the University of Windsor. He founded the *University of Windsor Review* in 1965 and was Editor until 1987. He is the author of five collections of short fiction. *Grace Notes: New and Selected Poems* is his fourteenth collection of poetry. McNamara is Professor Emeritus in the English Department at the University of Windsor. He lives in Windsor with his wife Margaret.

CONTENTS

ONE: GRACE NOTES

TWO: IMAGINARY FRIENDS

THREE: BACK IN THE REAL WORLD

One:

GRACE NOTES

Who that has heard a strain of music feared then lest he should speak extravagantly any more forever?

—Thoreau

FOUR LAST SONGS

(after Richard Strauss)

1.

A woman stands on the
shore of an autumn lake
singing across dead leaves
riding on the chill waves—

I am on the other shore
listening to words which
rise and fall in the wind—

I think the words are *goodbye*
sleep and *dark*—

2.

What was it I wanted
to hear?

Words that soothe crooned
low over the small waves—

And the singers voice rises
from deep in the lake where
the drowned sing in concord—

I bend to the waters edge
in this startled night—

And a bell deep sunk sounds
down there rocking in the deep—

3.

Rainwet trees hold summers
last leaves and the bell
can never cease—

I dream snow falling into
the lake and the wind
smells of snow the words
forever and *night* are
sung long and high—

4.

Now small birds sing
in the trees shaking
the rain down—

What was it I wanted
to hear?

Words crooned low over
small waves—*autumn night
come to me*—
before I sink to sleep—

PLAINSONG

They are cooking mash
at the distillery today
and white gulls drop
down to the water next
to the tall silos—

We drive through steam
clouds come out at the
bend in the river and
tall buildings over
there hold afternoon
light—

And the white silos the
rivers casual bend birds
circling sailing down
ships passing there—

Behind the bridge is sky
Behind the sky is a word

LISTENING TO THE TCHAIKOVSKY PIANO CONCERTO

I am eighteen again and play
the 78 rpm records on the small
turntable in my parents house
turning it down when my mother
asks me to—

I am waiting for life to happen
to me instead my father dies
and the last record ends—

This is not what I wanted
I say to the needle which
oscillates in a sinuous arc
hissing to itself after the
last swaggering chord—

A comment—a threat—
a promise—or just some
passing noise like the cars
outside our house on their
way someplace purposeful
in their going—

So long another music says
Its been good to know you—

SONG OF THE EARTH: MAHLER

Rain blown rose petals
on the sidewalk as if
thrown for a bride—

I knew the woman who
pruned those roses—

I followed her coffin out
into a wet morning—

Nobody to cut the roses
now last years leaves
crouch under the rotten
fence and the hawthorn
tree raises thin perilous
branches and the forsythia
bush is on fire in this
morning—

THE HOUSATONIC AT STOCKBRIDGE

For Charles Ives

You made me yearn for places Ive never been:
camp meetings hymns at dusk a river brown
as ale pouring itself over stones I cannot
touch

You took me to that place where the river
bends like an elbow leaning on a trains
window ledge

I thought of trains in the night passing
and a baseball glove hung up curling
to hold the hollowspace where the ball
is slung

I became a man in a straw boater walking
beside the river a woman on my arm shy
and fervent bending her face away from
the words I said

You hold me in that hollowed space
like shaking air

RODRIGO: CONCIERTO DE ARUNJUEZ

As a diver on the edge gathers all his forces in, uncoils and is launched higher than he can reach, tries for the top of the air, then falls in a poised gesture of acceptance to the falling and the water, the music allows no extra gesture. It is a pain that enters itself, fills itself up so that there is no room for anything else. A face which has never seen a mirror says something so simple you forgot to listen. Then you say *what* but it has passed will not speak again. A pain turned in on itself, a dry ache, no tears, words which can not be said, a music that hurts.

DEBUSSY: QUARTET IN G MINOR

First Violin:

A bush full of starlings
November Sunday afternoon
bent and huddled—

Second Violin:

Birch trees in startled light—
Grace abounding—

Viola:

Stately grave procession
sacred thing held up—
voices rise *ave ave*—

Cello:

The colour of a leaf-layered
path beside this somber river—

Grace abounds hovers over
the spent world—

ave ave—

MOUNTAINS AND RIVERS WITHOUT END

Summer light on the river
moves and from far across
from steeples and mountains
come songs our fathers loved—

Mountains and rivers without end!

In the meadow by the river
girls will wash their hair
dry it in summer light and
toss it to the wind so it
will smell like a sailors
coat and the river flows
dark and brown and somber
as it falls to shallows
and the sea—

Mountains and rivers without end!

In the autumn evening there
is mist on the hills and songs
across the river are over the
hills and far away—

Mountains and rivers without end!

We stand in all weather
put out our hands to test
the air—there is early snow
on the gravestones and we
look up at the barn on the hill
and something takes us
by the throat—

the harvest—

Mountains and rivers without end!

SATIE

A woman dances by herself
in a dim afternoon room
slowly turning slowly
bending hesitates—

A man on a train sees
her as the train slows
for the curve just past
her window seen swiftly—

His train had come into
the city past old yards
full of hollyhocks and
morning glory on fences—

Remembers walking at noon
in a foreign city all the
shops shuttered he walked
alone in high silent light—

Everything slouched together
at the end of the street
where he did not want to go
and a dandy came swaggering
around the corner wearing
a flower in his lapel—

FROM THE NEW WORLD

Dvorak came to America
four hundred years after
Columbus—

Dvorak saw Hoboken and
Cincinnati and Omaha
and Spillville, Iowa—

Dvorak saw the Mississippi
and said *Crikey!* when he saw
Niagara Falls—

Freud and Jung boarded
the *George Washington* in
Bremen in 1909 and set
out for New York to bring
psychoanalysis to the
natives—Freud fainted
before the boat sailed—

Ravel listened to jazz
in Harlem with Gershwin
and saw Edgar Allen Poes
house and Niagara Falls
and did not say anything
and saw the Grand Canyon
and did not faint—

DVORAK

There they are, the men in
heavy suits and slouch hats
the heavy men with beards
in 1909 dancing gravely—

At times the music is slow
sometimes quick but always
tender, restrained like
a mothers hand on a childs
sleeping face—

The men are heavy like the
names of Bohemian food they
are like me walking with my
granddaugher who rushes at
everything—I move slowly—
I see the world full of sharp edges—

I want to be one of the men
the bearded men in Prague
in 1909 wearing heavy suits
and slouch hats who dance
to grave music—

ADAGIO

My voice turns like a key
rusty in an iron lock today
the radio is playing Albinoni
and I am staring out the
window at snow melting on
the garage roof where a cat
probes a tarred patch

Yesterday I rode the up
escalator watched the down
escalator fall endlessly
endlessly stairs pass like
song rising or falling and
today

on the screened-in front
porch winter light falls
on indoor-outdoor carpeting
light falls on white wicker
and Albinoni turns slowly

Out there steam rises from
the garage roof the cat has
lost interest in the patch
and is now intent across
the yard and metal stairs
are rising rising falling
falling like songs

FOR ROY ORBISON

The Specific Shapes of Loss

A boat was heading upriver trying to beat the ice
a gull was diving again again again swooping down
no luck swept up again on sunstruck white wings

The clouds closed again like an eyes wink and
the cars on the drive were incessant orderly
barely held in check all intent on their way
some place everyone specific and alone—

None of this meant a damn thing after I heard—
something just left the world the way people
leave a room called away for some important
thing the way a movie screen goes dark—

I held the drab day in my hand held it tight
nobody said the word *lonely* like you did—
now I open my hand find it full of nothing

I think of lonely men in bars staring at the
air in front of them listening to music they
didn't pay for don't especially want wonder
where they'll go next someplace they've never
been to now I hold the day as pure as your
words—

The diving gull breaks the water again again
my fogged up windshield is hit by sudden sun
light just as suddenly goes dark again and
in that moment all the windshields on the
drive were sunstruck open and I said *for ever
green*

Fifty-Two Pickup

A cruel grownups joke *hey kid*
want to play fifty-two pickup?
and then the four suits jacks on kings
a pack of lies thrown all over—

Those hard lessons of childhood—
being bullied shamed full of
fear all that hard stuff
to learn how to grow how
to love and live with loneliness—
fifty-two someone says *thats*
not so old—

Too soon I say looking
at everything spilled on
the floor waiting to
be picked up

Level Crossing

The year has turned and I wait at the level
crossing cn cn norfolk and western cn cp erie
Lackawanna Illinois Central for weeks now
I could not listen to your music it hurt cn
cn b & o chessie now I slide the tape in and
remember all the places filled with your song:

Kozaks tap the awcommon inn domas place the
6511 club pete ryans buddys lounge the q t
the ambush and the red lion the pass time
the billy goat the two eighty seven the
melody and mickeys midget café the keg room
the holiday house mother mckennas pinocchios
kys knotty pine inn duffys the horseshoe
the starlite room and the chatterbox—

Detroit toledo and ironton bangor and maine
santa fe cn cn great northern southern pacific
and the caboose the train is gone the tracks
are clear and I can go anyplace I want
I sit for a minute the cars behind me are
impatient I don't know where to go

Holding a Good Hand

Another day: I stand in steel winter light
and stare at the empty river cant think of a
thing to say think I will remember this day
if I live through it as a big empty thing—

A boat passes me a high iron wall of rust
shutting off the skyline a big hand raised up
I raise my own hand to it say *here take this
its all Ive got*—

The boat is past me now left me astern its
wake slaps the shore the river settles back
down and I think of the way a field fills up
with night and tree lines hunch down flocks
of birds rising from them and returning like
scattered words in a song you gave me *here*

Is a gift you said *take it* and I held your
word in my hand the way a field holds the dark
the way birds lift the trees and I open my
hand hold it up again your word rises from
my hand to the dying light

MATINS

Bells in faroff steeples
summon and birds announce
morning—

bellsong birdsong—

Come and walk with me my
love listen to what my eyes
sing to you: I will not
let you go—

As a man carries a glass
of water to his child in
the night—not a drop will
fall the bough will not
break we shall gather at
the river—

Remember the dry light
over the ocean and the
long grass in morning
light and wild ponies
running on the beach
plunging in the surf
their manes shaking
in the wind?

Remember the prairie
swift seen between
the freight cars?

The prairie will be there
when the trains long gone
the ponies will be there
when we return—

Here are trees shaking
swaying in the wind and
staying in calm silence—

Train horns in the hills
the hoarse muttering of
the river where it falls—

What I hold in my hands—
not a drop will spill and
the bough will not break
and we shall gather at
the river and I will not
let you go—

THREE HORSES: A SONG FOR JENNIFER

We came when spring snow
lay on your lawn and you were
small as a sparrows heart under
that snow—

The river ran dark and chill down
from the mountains and we gave
you three horses:

the golden horse of the sun
the silver horse of the night
and the white horse of sleep—

You rode the horse of sleep
and the snow seeped reluctant
and clouds hung on the mountains
fleece caught on thorns and
the horse of sleep went across
that far field—

Now we are home and I listen
to music:

night keeps all your heart—
who can say—
only time—

My sparrows heart you
are not here and my arms curve
to hold you

only time—

The river still runs and horses
run in the dark and the white
horse is running in the rain
filled fields of sleep—

And you are home sleeping
and dream my holding you—

Two:

IMAGINARY FRIENDS

Dreams are funny things.

Burt Lancaster in *Brute Force*

A way of certifying experience, taking photographs is also a way of refusing it—by limiting experience to a search for the photogenic, by converting experience into an image, a souvenir. Travel becomes a strategy for accumulating photographs.

Susan Sontag

HISTORY OF FRANCE IN MODERN TIMES

Everything in France happened
In the Thirties avant le second
guerre

Jean Gabin smoked and
shrugged weary shoulders

Simone Signoret crossed languid
legs at Foquets corner of
Avenue Foch and the Champs
la petite glass of Calvados
on her table a cigarette
smoldered in the ashtray

At night the Citroens careened
and les flics burst into dives
where le jazz hot played
and Josephine Baker misbehaved

In the Foreign Legion they
ate beaucoup soupe drank
vin rouge and smoked

The rising smoke wrote in
art nouveau script above them:

La glorie—

TOURISTSPEAK

Good morning good afternoon
Good evening. How are you?
Is this your wife sister son?
How far is it to the museum
postoffice airport? How much
is a taxi? I am hungry thirsty
fatigued. How much is dinner?
This food is unacceptable.
Please give my shoes to the
chambermaid. Is there a doctor
dentist barber nearby? Hello.
These are not my shoes. My shoes
are brown. Goodbye.
We are departing.

ELEGY FOR MARIE WINDSOR
(Died Dec. 10, 2000. Aged 80)

"I didn't know we were doing film noir. I thought they were detective stories with low lighting."

—Marie Windsor

Your eyelids drooped like a tropical flower
a deadly one—

Your pouting lips looked as if they had
just been kissed hard or slapped—

"You'd sell your mother for a piece of fudge"
Sterling Hayden said—

You lived in that city that never slept
high heels on wet night sidewalks
lovely but deadly—

"She's a dish" Charles McGraw said
*"a sixty cent special with poison
under the gravy"*—

tough broad
dame
vixen
vamp
trollop
tramp
floozie
no man's moll

black lace stockings
slut stuff harlot stuff—

We in the popcorn dark knew:
sex was dangerous

the glittering allure of
cheap thrills
torpedo tits under
cashmere—

Marie there is no more sin—
we saw you in honkytonk neon
and now you are gone
leaving us in innocent sunlight
to say this:

*"Marie, Marie, hold on tight—
and down we went—"*

THINGS I LEARNED AT THE MOVIES

Never wear your galoshes in the movies. It is bad for your eyes.

When people in the movies go shopping they always buy celery or french bread. Even if they dont want dont like dont need celery or french bread they buy it and it sticks up out of a brown paper bag and when they arrive home the phone will be ringing and they will juggle the bag grope for the key and they wont make it in time. The phone stops ringing.

The apartment—*all* apartments—are furnished with ferns and framed movie posters. Evidence of passion: slow lingering trail of clothing from front door to bedroom (male and female clothing.) Fear of commitment: one lover will wake in the furtive dawn and go back up the trail of clothing to sneak out. A nearby beach will be provided for solitary walking and thoughtful brooding. A dog may be provided for chasing the stick thoughtfully thrown.

Some of these people came from vigorous ethnic working class roots. This is indicated by a return home, bantering with hot dog vendor or owner of sidewalk ethnic store and the gift of a melon. Or there is a vigorous ethnic wedding where all the women wear too much makeup and the men are combative and loud.

The people with the ferns and the movie posters return to their renovated brownstone and listen to an aria from *La Wally*. This is constantly playing.

Secret agents meet at the children's zoo. A child's ball will roll up to the rezident's feet. He will kindly roll the ball back to the child. We will hear the word *terminate* under the music from the carousel.

The laughing beautiful young people will leave the prom and go into the deserted amusement park. The amusement park will be no fun. We see all this from the inside of a hockey mask.

Perhaps the couple listening to *La Wally* will make love in front of the fireplace where all the celery and bread is burned.

And do not have car trouble in a small town. You will be raped or given over to satanists.

In the isolated mansion in the storm when the lights flicker and the butler announces that the bridge is out—

Never wear your galoshes in the movies

THE VIEW FROM THE WOODS

I always wanted to build out here
a small cabin between my woods and lake

My shops in town though and it would take
travel time—but

Just think how fine it would be to
wake in the spring and the trees full
of leaf and birdsong and even in snow—
(our winters get fierce you see and the
lake freezes solid) to wake and hear
the trees soughing—

Just the other night I was out here
as usual walking in my woods and he
came along—that farmer fellow who
fancies himself as a poet—there he
was gaping at my trees thinking some
thing poetic I suppose and then
went on to places he had to get to
leaving me back here alone and
I could hear the harness bells a long
way off and the only other sound
my own breath and wind in the trees-

I knew he had not seen me
I was deep in my woods
I was in a place I wanted to be
dreaming of my cabin and my trees—

Even a shopkeeper has to dream—
comes with the territory—

HIBISCUS

Bloomed in the courtyard
of the Oakwood Apartments

There was the unending moan
of traffic on the freeway

Someone walked through
the courtyard heels echoed
on the walk then silence
again a distant door closed

On tv across the pool faint
delighted laughter rose and
bloomed

The hibiscus didn't listen
drooping open as kissed
lips in the fragrant dark

DEATH BY MISADVENTURE*

(*Headline in Brighton *Argus*
  on death of Malcolm Lowry)

First of all Ripe is a funny
name for a place even in
Sussex and its hard to
get down to a little road
through tall hedgerows
the little rental car scraping
the verge

And the place isn't much—
a church a pub the grave
yard overgrown

gravediggers on strike

After signing the book
in the church step out
in late afternoon light
a jumble sale behind
the church

nothing much there

Well I say to the woman
behind a table *a famous
Canadian poet died here—*

She makes ah um noises
Drank himself to death
I say

Well she says *this
is a good place to do that—*

STUDS LONIGAN

Didn't take crap
put in lots of corner time
wondered if he should
sock it in—
caught a dose
didn't like Negroes
didn't call them that
boozed and whored
had a bum ticker
died young
died dumb

AT THE *SHAW* MEMORIAL

In the St Gaudens bas relief
resolute troops and Shaw
upright on his horse the winged
figure above them all go where
they must—

They are steeped in bronze
caught in midstep cannot look
back or down only go where
they are looking go where
they must—

The horse raises one foot
forever—

BACK ON THE GROUND

I stood at the top of the high
steps looking out—the lake
was chilled blue the sky full
of sky the white clouds on the
horizon white as mainsails—

Time was as wide as the steps
and the girl down there at
the stone balustrade looking
out at the boats was pulled
by the wind her hair blazing
white and blue excursion
boats traversed the lake and
the girl turned to walk away—

It was like music or a word
in me that broke everything
hollowed in me and I wanted
to go down the steps I wanted
to stay where I was and so
I turned to see the fountain
water flung up like diamonds
in noon light I drank in the
air like cold water—

PEORIA, 1927

In downtown Peoria you could
fry an egg on the sidewalk at noon

It hasn't rained for a month
and morning smells as soggy
as room 302 in the Olinger Hotel
where a textbook salesman groans
and turns over to find last
nights whore has left already

She carried her shoes out
to the hallway pulls them on

The elevator operator yawns
pretends not to be interested
as she steadies herself against
the wall to raise a foot to a shoe
he gets a whiff of knee as she
smooths her skirt down he opens
the gate *down?* he smiles
she doesn't smile back why
should she he aint the paying
kind of fellow—

A month ago it rained so much
the river overflowed and a boy
fell down a sewer was shot into
the river he did not survive——

Now the sewers are hollow dry
aching for rain

Miss Hewitt raises both arms
to push the hair off her neck
sighing thinks of Mozart and
that salesman who must be married

of course and all the boys
in the eighth grade classroom lean
forward to watch Miss Hewitt
and the slow pulse in her neck

A fat blue fly bumps at the
window screen the empty corn
stalks in the fields hang limp
the salesman dreams of water
tunneling under him
a woman comes out of
the Olinger Hotel walking
slowly into the hot day

Everyone agrees: its going
to be a scorcher

DESTINATIONS

From my place under the bridge I could
look up and think about the stories
of people flinging themselves off
hanging themselves oh all this long
ago back when people went crazy in
the winter blew their heads off with
gunpowder fed arsenic to the family
ran off with salesmen went to Chicago
turned trollop my aunts spoke of all
this in whispers hoping to shield me—

Dennis and I made our First Communions
I tried not to have sinful thoughts
hoped I would not forget in the middle
of the night take a drink of water
and a fine rain was falling I had a
terrible urge to stick out my tongue—
Marie Alice demure eyes downcast in
front of me I thought of her mothers
iron cooling on the board at home
all over town irons standing on boards
cooling—

Illinois you were a thorn in my heart

Out near the towns edge I pumped gas
at the Texaco read Thomas Wolfe all
night yawned all day some nights could
not stand it said *oh lost!* and swam in
the night river so different from the
simple placid creek in daylight we
skipped stones across sat under the
bridge listened to cars rumbling over
on their way to Joliet or further but
at night the river had no bottom my
skin shrinks and crawls as I remember

Dennis wondered if taking stuff from
the dime store was a mortal sin we
wanted war dreamed of war in that
summer and Dennis drowned in that
river

I loved the movies with wet sidewalks
after rain neon lit high heels click
echoed skirt flicking above the puddles—
in a room above the street I lay on
the bed curtains hung tired out neon
flicks I lie smoking of course staring
at the ceiling of course not looking
at the woman in the black slip curled
asleep at my side my eyes are on
something distant about to be shown
in flashback

So I grew up watching those exciting
fast girls in my class—Tillie Dolly
Lolly—all those names ending in
teeth clenched groin clenched *eee*
like cousin Susie all beautiful and
out of reach Susie posed under a tree
flowering in Uncle Buds back yard

I learned useful things from Uncle Bud
watched him frown at the thermometer
snap a skeptical finger at it *ninety
two? not hardly—*

Uncle Bud beat his wife everybody
said so he told me to be a man I
remembered it when the doors clumped
shut outside the church the day of
his funeral it was ninety-five in
the shade

Once listening to truck loads of
hogs cross the river heading north
to the yards I alone remembering
Dennis and a bus went across kids
yelling out the window at me
and a girls face smiling down they
had been to Lincolns tomb and
she was bored out of her mind rolling
her eyes at Vera dying for a smoke
the guide told them for godssake what
kind of marble and how goddam much
and who was that boy down there—
the girl on the bus would be named
Dolly or Susie or Tilly—

I remember a winter when the pipes
froze and the small plane crashed
and sadness spread like a stain
from Clear Lake Iowa

That winter I met a girl whose name
was not Susie or Dolly—

Out near the Des Plaines River we
parked it was in public private
and dangerous all around us the red
eyes of taillights staring we groped
and fumbled to radio light the music
full of our deep shallow breathing

We rose from the seat ready to come
back into the public world and the
forms of children not yet born whined
in back of us asking for fast food
asking for promises to make chances
to take charging the high price of
loving

Just the other day I thought *the*
ship is given to darkness and the
sea and I remembered Dennis and my
Uncle Bud and Shorty is dead and
Stash lives in Florida and Knudsen
is in the Golden Valley Nursing
Home and Dolly and Susie are god
knows where and my children are
grown and gone and I wonder if
the river still runs under the bridge

AS IMPERCEPTIBLY AS GRIEF

There is nothing to say
nobody to hear it still
my hands move rigid
I try for final words—

We kissed in the shadow of
the Moody Bible Institute
we were shameless—

Then her thin arms desperate
around me the tough traffic
went by on Torrance near
112th her arms close as
Stateline Road the August
sun was crazy as traffic
everything shook blazing   .
car radios on too loud—

Now I think of her lying
on a hill beside the river
and hunger as she did

Nothing will ever happen
again for her for the first time

I will walk near the night
river I want to call her name
I don't know her name

A friend said *hey forget*
it shes only a piece of ass
he said *put her there* and
shook my hand—

My Sunday sunburned girl
you were more
you were more
I know this now

I do not know your name
I did not put you there

LIVE ALL YOU CAN

Henry James sat high in the back of
Mrs Whartons motor car eyes big and
ready to take in every morsel of Rye
and environs mufflered to the nose
ready to see every thing the way poor
Strether saw the French countryside
as if through a gilt frame like the
one he remembered in a dealers window
life seen as if through a frame of art

Take poor Strether falling in love
over an omelette *aux tomates* and
strawcolored Chablis love was this
complicated thing James might have
said to Mrs Wharton as they putt-
putted along sex was difficult too
she might have answered she did not
inform him of her plans—

Back in London after dining with James
and after he left for his club the thing
happened: *The tryst—*

Edith Wharton was fortyseven when she
committed this first act of adultery
married for twentyfive years to poor
dull Teddy—

The act took place on the fourth of June
1909 in Suite Ninetytwo of the Charing Cross
Hotel a railway hotel with lots of quick
coming and going her lover was a cad who
went on to solace other women in other
hotels it was reputed that he solaced men
also he was not particular whom he solaced—

Well James might have told her *comme
il faut* do not be *a ficelle* in your
own life—

Life was not art sex like love was
complicated and sex like art was
not all it was reputed to be—

Take the sea he might have gestured
high in the motor car high above the
town and the coast all that coming in
and going out ceaseless not like poor
we whose coming and going had its firm
beginning and its promised end—

O charming Mrs Wharton might have said
charming and she might have meant it—

AT LOUIS SULLIVANS GRAVE

What had I come to see?
What did I expect to find?

Nearby tourists pose in
front of the Getty Tomb
and outside on Clark Street
a beer truck finds a spot
in front of the Kozy Tap
where architects on high
stools negotiate the
long afternoon and a girl
in a summer dress walks
between truck and tavern

The silence of the men
watching her follows
down the street like
someone sighing and far
to the west of here
where I put pennies on
the railroad track to
make them thin—I was
a boy—now men lift
the glasses with shaking
hands I am not a boy

The tourists are gone
The girl is gone into
green summer light

Once I dreamed that girl
came to me in the rain
to say smiling *forgive*—
I had been stern as music
I took her in my arms—

What did I expect to find?
Now I wish I had those
thin coins

ATGETS GARDEN

I climb the crumbled steps
touch the lichened stone
and my eye hunches down
an avenue of bare trees

Beyond the balustrade
is the hollow throat
of a bare fountain and
leaves on the steps are
flung like opened letters
on a table top nobodys
home I say to the rain
stained face of a statue

At the end of the avenue
of trees Proust stands
at attention the way he
did after seeing Vermeers
View of Delft: hat and
cane at his side—

Slowly Proust bows to me
and I return the salute

Between us the autumn
grass is like a hand held
out in any weather

I feel as if someone has
just or is about to arrive

And everything is full of
emptiness and I stand
like stone or a man staring
at the shining roofs of a
town in a painting all gold
in summer light

IN THE GULLY

I am in the gully
close to the sparse
shards of spring snow
brown spikes of last
years weeds scraps
of old tough flaked
newspaper and

Across the stark field
my house hunches inside
its new grey siding and

Inside the house my wife
hums *I fall to pieces*

A print hangs in the
living room: three
intelligent eyed horses

A black and white rerun
is on tv a laugh track
of the dead rises—

Beside the house forsythia
urges itself and at school
my son is safe and learns
social studies the print of
the horses heads was
my grandmothers now

The light slants lower
across the field and my
windows are on fire

My son is learning long
division

Soon the light will fail
and I will see the lights
of homecoming cars my son
coming home to learn that
geography is more than
distance and I will lie
down to wait for stars to
wheel and wink

In the orchard the trees
raise sleeping branches
free of last harvests
burden the grass is free
of crushed windfalls and
everything is waiting to
begin again

I am learning long division

I am in the gully
close to every thing
I love

RUSSIA

Leo Tolstoy appeared to me in a dream
large in his fur coat and large beard—

I thought you were Trotsky I said
That often happens in Russia he said—

It is the Nineteenth Century it is
always the Nineteenth Century in Russia—

Samovars bubble sleds are pursued
by wolves children are hurled off the
backs of sleds and Raskolnikov sharpens
his axe and the Samovars bubble all night—

A loaf of bread is just a few kopeks but
nobody has the kopeks and nobody
bakes bread—As the samovars bubble
all night nobody sleeps all night they
tell stories sipping tea through lumps of sugar

Everybody has three names everyone
gets three wishes and I ponder: how many
yersts from the Count de____'s house
to the village of N——?

Siberia is full of saintly sinners and finally
someone is born in 1900—

I ponder his photograph (1900—nothing)
he wears a workers cap and a moustache

He is flogged with a knout and sent to
Siberia which is full of saintly sinners—

Last night Trotsky appeared to me in a dream

You aren't Tolstoy I said—

It's still the Nineteenth Century he said

Tolstoy and Trotsky don't seem to have
three names—

Where are my three wishes?

Rodian Romanovich Raskolnikov
sharpens his axe—

His nickname is *Rodya*—

Thats four names—

This often happens in Russia

Three:

BACK IN THE REAL WORLD

Nothing gold can stay—

Robert Frost

In the yard I pray birds,
wind, unscheduled grass,
that they please help to make
everything go deep again—

William Stafford

THERE IS A FOUNTAIN FILLED WITH BLOOD

It began with melting snow
clumped on branches dropping
to fall pooling and

Seeking between and through
to fall swelling and this
aching hurl through a flume
all froth spume—

Now slow and clear and
I can count the rocks and
I put my hand into the water
cold as a bite into an apple
and I raise my shocked hand
to the tall sky and know
that I belong here—

I say there it is
and there it goes—

My mother sang a hymn in
the backyard as she hung
sheets—

The sheets bellied like sails
on ships going away—

CAITLIN

(for my granddaughter)

When you smile
all baroque composers
fall silent

Today you are far from
me and birds sudden
as thoughts fly from
the pear tree to the
forsythia bush and
the hard sky opens
says *here*—

Oh my small paratrooper
you dive into my life
and the sudden air hurts
to breathe

Nothing is promised
yet I feel hope spring
in me like swift wings

When you sleep your
eyelids are hummingbird
wings

ADAGIO FOR MARTIN

The garden is quick with the ecstasy
of birds and wind and light on leaves

A neighbors red towel flaps on a line
far off lawns are mowed and I hear the
pock of a distant tennis ball and in all
this music I sit holding my sleeping
grandson

I whisper his name—Martin—my brothers
name my fathers name and Martin is heavy
in my arms as I bend to look at his delicate
eyelids shut in reluctant sleep

The birds sing this slowly turning dance

Sun stunned trees hankering lawns
and the strawberries in their white
bowl and frail rinsed light

My father and my brother bow slowly
to us and we sink together like
rain in the river

SQUARE DANCING IN NAPERVILLE

for Dan Dungan

Forming the square you wondered
about the Quakers—about sex—
and you honoured her and dipped

If it feels good do it said the song
but you weren't sure as you
allemained whirling saw the
crash doors in the high school
gym with new varnish her
thighs under a sashay of bright
cotton and you led to the right
circled in a line and came on
back home and do-si-doed

Later in the hallway you looked
in at the dark machine shop
found the door open went in to
kiss among silent drill presses
circular saws hung on the walls
in moonlight *did you ever lie
and listen to the rainbow* echoed
from the gym your armpits damp
mouths open you kissed her

Well dan weve promenaded down
years pretty good since that
night you swung her in the circled
squares and bowed to her in the
hallway under the framed portraits
of Longfellow Bryant and Whittier

A boy in Danville broke my heart
she said and later going home on
the Chicago Aurora & Elgin late

you tried to remember the color
of her eyes all you could recall
was her hand on your forearm
the elbow swing the give of her
waist as you seesawed and wove
a ring and swung on through and
came back home

You broke her heart too dan—
the train doesn't run anymore
and if it did would it stop at
Naperville? its long since
Bob Dylan went electric and poets
had three names now my beard
is as white as theirs and I
haven't heard your voice for
a long time and still I honour
you in my mind where we sashay
back on home

FOR CHILDREN WHO DIED BY FIRE

(Our Lady of Angels School, Chicago, Illinois, 1958)

A father came to the ruin
three days after pounded
on the charred door called
come out son—Im here!
but his son has passed his
voice the son who jumped
and fell to stone—

In one room twenty-four
dead children sat silent
at their desks waiting to be
let go—

They are all gone past their
fathers voices now and the
Mass for the Holy Innocents
sung the coffins gone into
white winter sunlight—

The city held them awhile
then let them into darkness
the iron season turned and
Christmas trim and trees
were burned toys were lost
things broke down the decade
ended the world knelt down
waiting for new horror: men
who buried children in cellars
madmen on towers one dark
act followed another moving
into deeper dark—

I want to dream all children
back rising from the sidewalk
up into the burning air rising
to the windows and into the
rooms where fire hisses back
smoke draws into itself and
the childrens hands unfold
they are let go and down
they march backwards into
the yard back across the safe
street back safe to their homes
yawning breakfast back to bed
back to safe night sleep—

Now I call all fathers away
from the burned door say come
with me into this cold safe
night filled with sleeping
children—

The children do not fall but
are held up by their fathers
voices calling come out son
come home safe—

RUNNING RIVERS OF MY YOUTH
RUNNING RIVERS RUN

1

Out beyond the limits of my eye
the river came to me came and
went on past me intent in its
going towards what I did not
know running past my eyes limit

Stooping I put my hand down
to touch the sand bottom felt
the strange touch of far traveled
water

I learned to say it fingered
on a map learned said its name
but the river did not know
its name

I have known rivers since

The other rivers gave me far
places theyd been to and gone
those rivers at night running
secret and patient

Listen:
des plaines fox sangamon

I say the names to the dark
names strong as grass bent
gullied by their passage

2

Always I go back to that first
river of no name when I had
no name standing on cut gully
bank the large stones half wet
half white bone in dry light
knowing them sacred knowing
the rivers rill furrowing the
high certain field sacred
before I knew a name for my
self knowing my self whole

Somewhere beyond my limits
snow melted fell pooled
rivulets furrowed it began
patient gathering mining
down the sacred thing began

3

when the river froze over
and I stood on the sway
watching the waters skin
craze under my feet I was
out of bounds

In spring the river called
the shadows together in the
high field gathered the
scattered dark and the ice
broke and stately moved
down past my eyes limit

fox des plaines sangamon
gathering falling towards
sea

4

Once I stood in cold
shallows once I crossed
from rock to rock felt
the current coax and I
lay down in sunlit water
looked over the cut bank
at the high field

That field my mother rode
horses in the night the
barn burned and the wild
horses were driven out and
my mother rode them to the
river and across their manes
on fire

Listen once more:

the water clear as gods eye

My mother was a girl who
rode wild horses my father
was waiting in the city
they would meet in that
city I would wake in to
this world and wait for
rivers

5

Last night I woke to rain
thought of rain falling all
across my yard down my
street far across all down
the river falling into all
the rivers into that river
I named before I had a name

Thought of rocks split by
water the earth mined by rain
rushing falling water in the
dark as I lay listening to
that patient water fall and
I dreamed myself back rode
horses of fire back to the
first river

Listen again:

the water clear as gods
eye cut gully bank brown
casually said to me death
and forever far away close
to you closer than your
name

HEART LAND

—for Margaret

The geese in the park will not
migrate this winter—
they have forgotten how or why—

Its been months now since we
came home after thousands of
miles and two oil changes—

We kept stepping on the tracks of
Lewis and Clark and kept on crossing
the Missouri River over and over—

Have we changed at all?

There were those sheep in trucks
behind the Wranglers Café in
Wyoming mildly regarding us but
what could we do for them?

We had gone high on those
mountains and came down to sweet
water and a land full of sky—

Our squeegeed windshield let the
whole prairie into our laps and
a combine harvester in the Kansas
afternoon worried at the dry field—

Far from Alberta where we left our
son and far from Jackson where we
did not buy Million Dollar Cowboy
Bar tee shirts—

two regrets—

Far from spiked purple flowers
in the ditches of North Dakota
where sloughs crowded the roads
edge and the sky was wide awake—

If tomorrow comes and I wake to
find you next to me Ill know I am
home—

If tomorrow never comes again well
weve been there and back again—

You are the country I will never ever
fly from like geese in the park close
to home you are the map of far places
in my heart—

SNOW DOWN HOME

They tell strangers not to
try to get to the mailbox
in a storm many have tried
gone and died on the way—

That snow is confusing
like god gone nuts—

Come summer and corn
tassels hang in sunshock
you remember the snow
and almost miss it—

Take the hired hand who
showed up at harvest
time worked my uncles
field ate dinner with
the family didn't say where
he had been nobody asked—

After the harvest he up
and left next fall he
did not come back nobody
asked where he was where
he had gone—

Like someone who went out
in the blizzard trying
to find the barn or go
back home just went out—

THE WORLDS HUNKS AND COLORS

I am learning to love the world
again like a convalescent
released from care naked and
tentative walking slowly—

Carefully into it bereft
of companions already gone
into dark silence with no
word of comfort or goodbye—

They were the light of this
world the salt of it—

I will walk into the light
which gentles the worlds
hunks and colors so long
to the dark praise this
world fallen or uplifted
into light—

SIX PROSE POEMS

The Game of Marco Polo

It is played in the summer in the pool. There, beneath the
plum tree bent overripe, the children circled one. He calls
marco through his hands and a chorus *polo polo polo* sets
him into blind pursuit. Plums fall from the branches. I
must skim them out each day. August bends toward fall.
The voices of children still rise *marco* and *polo polo*.
Dusky plums forget the blossoms. The children dive
searching for something. I bite a plum. It tastes of winter.

The Yo Yo Man

When he came you knew spring was there at the edge of
the playground. He was thin in his big pants, his pockets
full of the exciting blue yellow and red wood. His face
was beyond smiling. Only his hands danced and the wood
spun out on the singing strand, hunching itself in to a
whirling grin. And the dog was walked, the baby was
rocked, we went around the whole green world and sank
down finally into our separate sleep. Then he went away.
I think of the man without a country drawing a map in his
cabin, imagining his native country, ignoring the blue
waves his ship passed through, fighting sleep, not walking
the actual dog on the ship's deck.

Doppler Effect

The machine in the soda fountain made a green pop
called *Green River*. On the machine was a picture of a
river moving away from you towards the horizon. The
light behind the picture made the river green shining
ripples as it flowed away from you. My brother liked
Green River. When I visit him in the locked ward he
speaks of it with some passion. Now I buy him magazines

which he will not read. I leave cigarettes for the attendant
whom I do not trust. On the highway home I am thinking
what next. I am calling *green river, green river* to all the
cars and the words fall down behind me. They fall down
like something collapsing in on itself, something lost in a
pocket, a river going no place special, but relentless
moving away, pouring through a hole at the edge of
the world.

In Chicago

In the factory called Sharp Tool I painted all the machines
gray. One of the machines was called CINCINNATI. Sharp
Tool was in Chicago. It was a place where they sharpened
industrial tools. What other kind of tools are there? I
thought as I painted the machines that sharpened the
tools. When I was painting over and over the raised letters
CINCINNATI, salesmen from Ohio were stacked in a hold-
ing pattern over the airport, looking down at Gary and
thinking *Chicago is dirty.* The landscape, I want to tell
them, allows us to say its shape. So I say *The landscape
allows us to say its shape.* Paint drips on the floor from my
brush. The Indiana dunes curve around the edge of the
lake like a slowly curving hand.

Home Movie

Meeting your wife at the pier. The doctor sent her on a
cruise for her health. She has met Louis on the ship. They
have been in love since the Captain's Ball. Both are decent
people and nothing has been consummated. A few kisses
near a lifeboat. Now here you are with flowers and all the
children. Louis watches the reunion from an upper deck.
He calls your wife's name but the ships whistle blows and
nobody hears it. Now you are all in a cab, the children are
talking. Louis follows, disguised. None of the children are
yours.

Urban Renewal

Today bulldozers press reluctant tree stumps. Shy roots pulled into the light, lie at last resigned. The houses like a row of kicked in teeth watch a young girl pass on her way home. The girl plans future grocery lists, garage sales, divorces. *The violated houses,* she thinks, *in a season of betrayals.*

THE SHAPES OF FIRE

1. The Fire of Torches

The villagers gather courage and march to the monster's castle, carrying torches. The creature fears fire. Lucky for us in the popcorn dark.

2. The Boy's Own Campfire

They tell lies and ghost stories. Behind their circled backs is large darkness. They crouch near the fire.

3. The Autumn Fires

Smell of burning leaves and the *punt* of a kicked football. The sound and smell of regret.

4. The Triangle Shirtwaist Factory Fire (1911)

Victims, mostly immigrant women, leaped to their death. A man the newspapers called *The Angel of Death* gallantly helped them step out into the burning air.

5. Fire in the Hole

In South Dakota they are blasting a mountain face. What remains will be a statue of Crazy Horse. Nobody knows what Crazy Horse looked like.

6. The Refining Fire

Gold shapes itself in the crucible, rendering, purifying, painful.

7. Angel Fire

He comes in the likeness of fire. Brightness puts out our eyes to this world.

8. The Fire of Creation

Dawn on the Outer Banks. Terrible as God's opening eye.

MAN IN THE SNOWY FIELD

A man walks in the field
between the lake and
apple orchard—

He is half way across
the field intent on where
he is going—

We are between
weathers chill but not bone
cold a weak light over the
iced lake low clouds
slumped down out there
and bare branches of
apple trees etch on
the sky—

The man is moving away
from the orchard across
the field which lies like
an opened letter—

I watch him go wonder
where he is bound and
I turn to my own life
where I am going—

LEARNING TO SEE

The yard across the street
is filled with snow and
looks like a Breugel painting
I saw in a book—

Sullen low country sky
peasants walking away
from me and the large
rump of a horse going—

All moving away and down
to a village where dogs
nip at the wheels of carts
and small people occupy
themselves carry trays
of bread bundles of wood—

A one-legged man leans
on a crutch staring at
bent backs of fishermen
on the bridge: foolish
fishermen bent over
a frozen river—

In spring the river is
gorged with fish gaping
to be caught—

None of this is in the
yard across my street—

Everything rushes to the
vanishing point: peasants
fishermen horses carts
houses a man leaning on
a crutch all gone—

The yard across my street
is full of snow and
nothing else—

I look and am content
with absence—

I am learning to see—

I SEE THE DARKNESS

—for Bob Doyle

We looked up into
late summer sky
light lingering—

Waited to be gathered
picked up gathered in
held up in angel air
this clear rapture of
evening—

Across the pale water
a trail of freighter
smoke at the horizon
then nothing—

*at your coming may
the martyrs receive—*

And we went in and
then out again in
the dark alone and
together—

I know that late summer
light will not come again—

may the angels receive—

Things left unsaid—

*in paradisum
deducant angeli—*

FOR ERIN

Always when I think
of you it is summer
and you are thirteen
and riding your bike

Your face has that
careful inward look
of poised caution

It breaks a boys heart
makes fathers hold their
breath and wonder whats
on your mind as you wheel
along everything holds
its breath—

Well you cant be thirteen
forever—

Boys know that and fathers
hold their breath let it
out slow wish it were not
so wish you would never
get down from your bike
lean it against a tree
everything begins to sigh—

I wish you would ride
forever thirteen down
our street in summer
light which never fades—

SAYING GRACE

for Jim Cooney

1

The dank air in the greenhouse
held its breath

The stretched plastic shivered
like pale silk in the early sun

Everything was ready to grow

And that was when we had the
late storm and I finally knew
you weren't coming back

You had gone leaving me
to tell the story

I never knew there was
a story to tell

2

Thirst is a word hard to say
comes out hoarse and parched

Now sitting in my kitchen
I look at two apples in
a bowl and a glass of wine
red as the apples

Outside dark branches crack
on themselves to let ice crusts
fall to the snow

Yesterday I made bread kneading
harsh rye and cracked wheat into
mild white flour thinking *blend
in tough*

Annual tree rings have grown
around the thought of you
deep in the hard wood

3

Thirst I say to the icy trees
and the bowl of fruit

It is early spring and new
storm sewers are angled
on the roadside waiting for
heavy equipment

Sirens far off come closer
and I think of my children

What can I tell my children
or all those I love?

Nothing is good enough for them

4

There is no story to tell
but I will say this for you:

I will say grace over this
bread and fruit and wine

Quench I will say and deep
inside me something breaks
and begins again

DIXON, SUMMER, 1943

I sat beside the gray filing
cabinets one drawer labeled
feeble-minded—

Oh no I thought *oh no*—

The nurse said my brother
had been agitated that
morning and there would
be no visit—

We went to the Black Bear
Motel where a chained
black bear paced and his
little eyes angry—

I swam in the Rock River
water black as the bear—

All night the jukebox in
the tavern across the road
played *Pistol Packin Mama*
and the black bear paced
and turned and paced his
chain clanking—

oh no my mother said

oh no—

DREAMING OF THE COLD WAR

Lately I dream Im in Russia
and its night and the streets
are empty and wet and its
snowing and I wait for a
streetcar everything is in
black and white—

Or its Munich after the war
all wet cobblestones and
sinister streetcars—

A woman comes up to me
whispers something in a
language I dont understand
her face wet with tears or rain
or snow—a warning? a plea
for help? a question?—

I stand there helpless and
then wake up to my own
world of light and color
a world where I am not
a spy and no woman weeps
or stands in the snow
waiting for a streetcar or
the police—

I walk in my common world
with no fear but somehow
I am homesick for Russia
or Munich—

Tonight I will go back and
dream I know the language—`

EFFULGENT

My grandson curls up
on the couch intent with
the fossil I have given
him—a delicate fish
caught in stone found
in a lake—

Forty-five million years
ago the lake did not
know it was in Wyoming—

It is hard to tell my grandson
about years—a million or
forty-five
or my age

The delicate fish is no help
patient lying in its stone—

My grandson's delicate eye
lash blinks slowly as he
sees the fish in its stone—
he *knows* this fish—

The moment is one of a
million hurrying ticks of time
here caught and full of simple
light—

Like the morning light here
or in Wyoming slowly
spreading spreading—

AGMV Marquis

MEMBER OF SCABRINI MEDIA

Quebec, Canada
2004